Praise for Jeral Williams'

Sunset Without Dawn

"*Sunset Without Dawn* offers a glimpse of one father's unfathomable loss. As Jerry Williams aptly assesses in his debut poetry collection, "Pain stabs in proportion to love." Williams transposes grief concerning his daughter into a series of poems that not only serve as a moving elegy but a deep well of healing wisdom. His words depict raw truths of parental devastation yet gift a sweetness of unending devotion."

> —Jennifer Grant, winner of the 2021 Blue Light Book Award for *Dangerous Women* and author of *Good Form.*

"Jerry's book of poems charts his heroic personal journey out of his deeply felt grief into a greater understanding of his learning to live graciously with his profound loss—his reader watches him intentionally pursuing and achieving a larger, reflective, self-aware, and self-critical stance—and a new and deeper understanding of self—his success is charted in his elegant poems etched in unflinching clarity and simplicity and sincerity—his poetry is fluent in an idiom rooted in Kansas and in his love and his embrace of the stoic values of character of his beloved American West—his lessons are homespun—prosaically expressed as—either you deal with grief or grief deals with you—you can't do it without love—tough love abides—his expression of the stoic values transforms the prosaic into the elegiac—a sad but at once an inspiring and uplifting music—bells for Jerry Williams' daughter—"

> —Tim Lally, Falls Church, Virginia.

"Jeral Williams is a poet with a deep consciousness. His words speak to the overwhelming storm of traumatic loss, the painful uncertainty death creates, and a world forever changed. Not stopping there, he writes through his grief and bears witness to grace—bringing courage and hope and a new dawn."

—Maryella Desak Sirmon, physician and author, Mobile, Alabama.

Sunset Without Dawn

Poems by Jeral Williams

Negative Capability
PRESS
MOBILE ALABAMA

Sunset Without Dawn

Copyright © 2022 Jeral Williams.

Book and cover design by Cristina Delgado-Howard. Cover design features an edited image of Albert György's Mélancolie. This image was originally posted to wikipedia by Flickr by art_inthecity at https://flickr.com/photos/57286185@N04/44551153491 (archive). It was reviewed on 6 May 2019 by FlickreviewR 2 and was confirmed to be licensed under the terms of the Creative Commons 2.0 Generic license.

Published by Negative Capability Press
150 Du Rhu Drive, #2202
Mobile, AL 36608
www.negativecapabilitypress.org

Dedication & Forward

Shelle Dawn Williams Tilstra was born May 25, 1964. She lived 37 very active years until her tragic death in 2001. My writing is an expression of pride in an extra-ordinary daughter, our sorrow for her loss and my attempt to honor her.

Jeny, my wife, and I came through this tragic loss together. I thank her for her love and compassion. This book is dedicated to Jeny.

Our sons brought us joy; our family and friends, too numerous to mention, gave us strength in the grieving process and I thank them.

I thank Cristina Delgado-Howard and the staff of the Negative Capability Press for their work and my friends in the WIN Workshop for their friendship and support. In particular I express my appreciation to Tim Lally, colleague and friend, for his mentoring of my venture into poetry, to Maryella Sirmon for providing excellent advice and support in the process of bringing the book to fruition and to Dr. Sue Walker for her teaching.

Grieving occurs in many ways. I hope my expression of joy for our daughter and of my pain for her loss bring strength and solace to others.

Acknowledgements

The title phrase "Mourning into Dancing" was taken from a book by Henri Nouwen, "Turn My Mourning into Dancing", <u>Thomas Nelson</u>, 2004.

"Two Urns Sit on the Shelf" was a personal poem written for fellow poet, Maryella Sirmon, and her husband honoring the loss of their son, published with her permission.

"Magnificence of Nothingness" was published in <u>Stormy Pieces</u>, <u>Mobile Writers' Guild Anthology</u>, Fall, 2021.

"Hands of Reflection" was published in the <u>Birmingham Arts Journal</u>, Summer, 2021.

"Livin' with Peace" was published in the Alabama Writers' Cooperative <u>Awarded Writers Collection</u>, 2021.

"Sumo Bout with Doubt" was published in <u>Agape Review</u>, November 27, 2021.

"In the Rose Garden of Musée Rodin" was published in <u>The Opiate</u>, vol. 27. Fall, 2021.

Table of Contents

I

A Father's Darkest Moment

Salty wet on sallow cheeks

crawls wrinkles to my beard.

Dampness stroked in musing;

her birth engraved in granite,

her death, the laser ever shining.

Quilt squares post her life,

shrouding death's morbid mask

hidden deep beneath life's layers.

I do not look often,

I do not look willingly.

I occasionally glance

and always shed a tear.

<h1 style="font-family:cursive;text-align:center;">A Dawn Observed</h1>

I prod heart's edges;

memories of love flow,

some red, some green, some brown.

Her reflections, ever green, bring joy,

an airport embrace, a last little wave.

Haunting memories shine red.

Bittersweet brown in her children's faces

deepens my loss

and celebrates her life.

Independent, competitive,

she fought with her brothers, but as she grew,

used her gifts for others.

Thoughtful, she visited, sent pictures and cards,

brought cross-stitch joy.

Determined, she took a back seat to no man or
woman.

She was a good wife, mother, sister, aunt and friend.

I Remember

Topeka, Kansas (1964-1966)

I remember

    her birth, more painful for her mother than her brothers' births.

I remember

    her having no hair until she was two.

I remember

    her complaining her socks and collars were "too tight."

I remember

    her hunkering in a basement for a Fujita 5 tornado.

I remember

    her hugging "My," a rag of a night blanket.

I remember

    her drawing lines in the backseat her brothers were not to cross.

Iowa City, Iowa (1966-1970)

I remember

    her hoarding Halloween candy.

I remember

    her cutting her own hair.

I remember

    her loving rabbits and pigs.

Normal Illinois (1970-1980)

I remember

her fighting a bully who picked on smaller children.

I remember

her as a high school student, explaining Base 2 to college students.

I remember

her learning to crochet and knit left-handed from a right- handed
mother.

I remember

her shooting hoops, playing golf, skiing.

I remember

her hiking, scenic drives and building a cabin in Colorado.

I remember

her gathering rock collections.

Mobile, Alabama (1980 -1983)

I remember

her being told simultaneous physics and chemistry courses were
too difficult.

I remember

her graduating Valedictorian.

I remember

her drinking too much before the state track meet.

I remember

her dawdling and picking over an expensive meal.

I remember

her organizing, preparing, accomplishing.

(1983-2001)

I remember

her being the first female physics co-op graduate student at her university.

I remember

her forgetting where she parked a rental car in Hughes Aircraft's enormous lot.

I remember

her enjoying a special wedding and reception.

I remember

her telling her mother not to visit her first granddaughter until bonding was complete.

I remember

her sending tapes of birthdays, holidays and grandchildren's lives.

I remember

her passing the Bar Exam for patents and trademarks.

I remember

her keeping up with the men drinking Sake in Japan

I remember

her cross-stitch gift, "A father is someone you look up to no matter how tall you grow."

A Portrait of Dawn

Self-Willed

Our decision to go to The University of Iowa graduate school with two children and a third child on the way required careful planning and big adjustments. The biggest adjustment was living in a 10-foot by 55-foot mobile home.

I knew nothing about the care of a trailer home and certainly nothing about preparations for cold Iowa winters. Jeny had the skill to balance a meager budget, command a household, care for young children, and perform her magic in 550 square feet.

Our bed filled one tiny bedroom. Early one morning, Dawn climbed into our bed. I awoke to see our young daughter with a scarf around her head. She announced she was ready to go to school.

A peek under the scarf revealed Dawn had cut her own hair. The action foretold a life of strong-will and personal discipline.

Generous

By any definition, we were poor economically. Many graduate students with monetary limitations lived in the trailer court. Our celebrations were inexpensive, some would say cheap.

Halloween was a special holiday in trailer court life. Creating costumes and buying candy took planning, creativity and sacrifice. Jeny accomplished everything and then ventured into the cold, to chaperone a miniature Hawkeye football player, a ghost, and a Batman.

I remained home and distributed candy to shy little elves, proud princesses, and bold cowboys.

Laughter and hot cocoa filled our small shelter when our children returned with abundant candy.

Dawn was a very organized, in-control person from an early age. She would take her candy and carefully put it in a box under her bed. She was reluctant to trade or share with her older brother. Days after his candy was gone, she still hoarded a stash under the bunk bed in the children's tiny bedroom.

One day I took all of her candy except one piece. That evening, I asked if I could have a piece of her candy. I hoped to teach her a lesson about generosity.

My four-year old went to her secret box and returned. With tears in her eyes, she held out her hand. "I only have one piece but Daddy you can have it." My heart melted. My lesson for her became a lesson for me.

Honor Her Father

Halloween was not the only celebration where Dawn's love taught me a lesson.

When we moved from Normal, Illinois to Mobile, Alabama, we bought a house before selling the old one. Two mortgages meant careful financial planning. Restaurant dining was not in the budget. When we sold the house in Normal, our family celebrated with a dinner at Constantine's Restaurant.

Dawn was a picky eater throughout her life. On our special night, she ordered an expensive dish and then picked and dawdled with the food.

She knew I was raised by depression era parents and our family did not waste food. She also knew this was an expensive meal. She did not want to displease me, but try as she may, the best she could do was pick little pieces and with great effort downed small bites.

Seeing the situation, in a fit of self-righteousness, I said, "If you are not going to eat your meal, give it to me. I will finish it." She passed the plate knowing I was displeased.

I took one bite and nearly threw up. The cheese was rotten. She had sat there all that time trying to eat to please me. I judged her for being a picky eater and never considered the food might be bad.

Once again, her love for me taught me a valuable lesson.

A Lesson in Teamwork

Occasionally I taught Dawn a lesson. She was a good runner and made running an important part of her life. In high school she was on the track team. Her school's relay team qualified for the Alabama State Championship.

For some long-forgotten reason, Dawn had too much to drink the night before the meet. She woke up feeling bad and did not want to go to the meet.

In fairness to her, she transferred from a school with excellent women's sport's programs to a school without excellent programs. She was not heavily invested in these new programs.

We discussed not going to the meet. I was adamant in my concern for her teammates. She was on a relay team. Not going was not about her, but about her team.

Dawn went, ran well and then "tossed her cookies." I was proud of her for meeting her responsibility.

Competitive

Dawn's competitive nature in sports carried over into her career. She was not going to be treated as a second-class person because of her gender.

In graduate school, Dawn was working on her Master's Degree in Applied Physics. When it came time for a co-op experience, she the first female accepted into the physics graduate co-op program at her university. She worked for Hughes Aircraft in Los Angeles.

Housing was expensive in Los Angeles, so Hughes owned several homes for co-op students. The first day of work, another student had a rental car and offered Dawn a ride to work. Along with three thousand other employees, they parked the car and hurried to get badges, go through orientation and begin the first day of work.

At the end of the day, Dawn and the driver returned to the lot and realized that in the excitement of the morning, they forgot where the car was parked. To make matters worse, neither could remember the make and model of the rental car. A long time was spent hunting though the huge lot before finally locating their car.

Her competitiveness meant she was deeply chagrined by mistakes. She could laugh at herself, but she did not enjoy being wrong. Dawn was deeply embarrassed at her mistake, but she shared her tale with us in good humor.

Emancipated

Sometimes Dawn's competitive nature and drive to be equal with men caused problems. She worked in the automotive industry. She was extremely successful in a male-dominated field. Her ability to know the technical language of scientists and engineers and be able to communicate to sales people and consumers contributed to her success.

Dawn had responsibilities for international activities and traveled to Europe and Asia. One problem with competitiveness arose in Japan. She called one day and asked if I liked Sake.

That was her way of beginning her tale of woe.

Dawn was in a meeting in Japan, and the host took them for a Japanese meal served while seated on pillows on the floor. As was the tradition, the Japanese drank and toasted frequently throughout the evening.

Dawn was not about to be outdone by the men, and so she drank right along with them. When she stood, she had a terrible time getting back to her hotel. Dawn had no idea of the power of Sake.

In Control

Dawn and Shawn's wedding and reception were grand affairs. She was married in a beautiful ceremony, marred only by the filming. The church required the film camera be set up in the balcony.

Later, when we viewed the film, I watched intently as the people gathered. As one of the last couples was ushered in, I remember thinking "Who is wearing a Yarmulke?" To my chagrin, I was that person. My bald spot was much larger than I realized and was reflecting the light.

The reception was a sit-down dinner. The Excelsior Band, the featured Mardi Gras band in Mobile, provided a lively atmosphere filled with laughter and dancing.

Dawn's organizational skills were evident as the events went off flawlessly. Behind the scenes, her need for control reached a crescendo with the lady preparing the cake. Dawn was in Minneapolis and the lady was in Mobile. Dawn regularly checked each detail of the cake. Finally, the cake lady called Jeny. She said, "Could you please tell your daughter, this is not our first wedding cake!"

New Beginnings

My wife, Jeny, had a much healthier relationship with her grandmother Myrtle, than her mother. Much of her model for being a woman came from Myrtle.

When other women her age were doing everything to cling to their youth, Jeny desperately wanted to be a grandmother. She hinted, cajoled, teased even begged. Finally, on a family cruise, Dawn got pregnant.

Jeny was a consultant to small hospitals around the country. Dawn and Shawn, were living in Minnesota at the time of the pregnancy. Jeny scheduled herself to be nearby in Wisconsin when the baby was due.

The week the baby was due, Dawn called Jeny. They had read a book and decided Jeny was not to come until they bonded with the baby. Jeny was disappointed but assured Dawn, she would be there as soon as possible after they bonded.

A very short time after Dawn came home from the hospital, Jeny got a call from Shawn. He wanted to know how fast she could get to Minneapolis. The baby was crying, Dawn was crying. She could not control the baby, and Shawn was near tears in frustration. They were as bonded as they were going to get.

Jeny arrived that day. As she walked through the door, both parents handed Jeny their new daughter Andrea, and said they needed to get away and have some space. They quickly departed. Andrea was fussy and Jeny set out to understand the problem.

When the parents returned, Jeny asked them if they had burped Andrea. The two physics majors looked at each and said yes.

Then Jeny put the baby on her shoulder and gave her a firm whack. Andrea gave such a loud brraaah our son-in -law thought their daughter was hurt.

The physics majors looked at each other again. Chagrined, they realized they had not burped the baby. Maybe Jeny was as wise as some books.

Andrea stopped fussing and Dawn talked to her mother almost every day the rest of her life.

Loud Words

The phone rang.

It was Dawn's husband.

"Hello Shawn"

"Hello Jerry.

It has been very foggy up here.

A trash truck ran a stop sign and hit Dawn on her way to work."

"How is she?"

"She's dead."

Silence invites mindfulness.

Dawn's memory knows no death.

Destiny is Not Always a Choice

A father's face shines, the nurses sigh,

baby girl born amid a mother's cry.

Her destiny marked by other's choices.

Loving daughter, mother and wife,

successful professional life,

died from another's negligence.

One Father's Lament

Pain

glides as an un-held wind.

Pain

rooted as a white oak tree.

Pain

stabs in proportion to love,

my wound vast and lasting.

Transient moments pass,

I seize her memories.

Her annual life my perennial loss

planted by negligence.

A fallen daughter's father knows empathy,

I will sting of her death forever.

Lasting Memories

The hearse poised in silence.

Bronze tomb in trembling hands approached.

Well-practiced somber tone inquired,

"Would you like to see her one last time?"

My respectful no, blanketed a screaming heart.

I prefer her last hug and smile

to an immovable casket pose.

A final look, sadness reigns.

I want images of joy:

Celebrations, hand-made Christmas ornaments

airport waves, birthday cookies,

her first date in heels.

Will we share a great beyond? Who knows?

I hope. I pray. I believe.

She loves me and I love her.

But for now, the final fire brought ashes

and her urn gathers dust.

Adrift

I drift through windy days.

Antiseptic gale of dread

howls to limp and shredded sails

my keel hauled; my ballast shed.

In time, slight tautness,

the canvas barely flutters,

the absent ache endures,

no anger, no rage, just sadness.

Agony swells within a father's void,

missed hugs and smiles

torture my voyage.

I rock powerless, without direction,

waves and tides my pilots,

no anchor for my sails.

Chasing Shattered Dreams

The worm fights the ants,

until the robin eats the worm,

lays a pretty blue egg the jay shatters;

all the king's men couldn't put it together again.

Death fractured hopes in a thousand shards

strewn wide across a mind.

Gathered into sparkling cairns,

her vision shines through the prism.

Absurd ambition kindled,

begins the search for edges,

chasing shattered dreams.

impossible to restore.

Transforming Ties

Death alters love's connections,
melts joy's bonds,
jolts anger and despair,
tightens links to emptiness,

sharpens memories of joy—
ornaments, gifts and pictures
celebrations, holidays and hugs good-bye—

gentles the tug of her son Kyle's voice,
her daughter Andrea's smile.

In the flow of time
despair and anger weaken,
joy grows,
emptiness haunts forever.

Meeting Measured Treasured Grief

"I measure every grief I meet"
— Emily Dickinson

before our daughter was killed
my milestones for death—
Mom and Dad and friends
expected pains in passing

the sadness
of parents in Grief
too wide, too deep
too steep an initiation

it hurts to live
without goodbyes,
watching deflects lightning pain
even so death is death

smiles come slowly
to grief experienced not observed
as long as the compartment
latch stays sealed

years have gathered
and still the memorial
rattles cages patching
shattered hearts

ache never goes away
I know it never will
our joy of living sons
overrides the pain

everyone grieves I pray
blessed are those who mourn
comfort comes to us
from near and far away

grief reflected in eyes
and posture of the sad --
deepest sunken in the air
of a child's death

a parent sees the pain
in others; and in the Father
not only death—
but conscious sacrifice

how deep the love
that for my life
He gave His only Son—
unfathomable to me.

My History is My Life

*"When the dung beetle moves know that something has moved it.
And know that its movement affects the flight of the sparrow, and
know that the raven deflects the eagle from the sky and that the
eagle's stiff wing bends the will of the Wind People, and know that
all this affects you and me, and the flea on the prairie dog, and the
leaf on the cottonwood."*
—Tony Hillerman. *The Ghostway*

History lives when I ponder:

life's actions large or small

alter matter, and matter.

Different history, different life.

If valiant volunteers from Maine

hadn't held Little Round Top,

would slavery's scourge be braced?

Different history, different life.

If God rewound history

and posted to Amazon Prime,

what would you choose to see;

Plato, Lincoln, or Jesus by the sea?

My choice, the morning our daughter died.

One second faster she lives;

what happened matters to me.

Different history, different life.

Turn My Mourning into Dancing

Book title from Henri Nouwen

Easy the morning dance when the world was begun.

Easy the dance of a firstborn son.

Easy a daughter's wedding dance.

Dancing death is difficult.

In darkness and silence

we waltz

bent in slowness and sorrow,

fused hearts drifting,

sifting our daughter's memories.

I yearn to dance New Orleans style.

Commence in solemn tone and walk,

stooped shoulders bearing burdens,

loss cast in requiem tune.

Trumpet, trombone, tuba, clarinet, and drum,

grave to andante,

until sunshine cracks the gloom.

In replanting light

joyful memories bloom,

fringed bumbershoots bask in tempo,

top hats nod and sway,

tambourines join the fray.

Black, gold and silver gain luster,

moderato to *allegro* to viva,

the saints march in,

the Second Line parades,

the caisson rolls on.

A Mother Knows

In gestation, bumps and kicks

spawn an awakening,

not her body alone.

Lifeline to another being,

a physical, visceral, eternal bond

no man will never know.

Cord cut,

a daughter growing,

a mother's vault of love filling.

Grandmother's advice—

"Raise her to live with someone else

from the day she is born."

I know Mom

wanted her to live with God,

just not so soon.

When our daughter was killed

a cord severed; a vault emptied

in a way a mother knows.

I hug, I hold

I share grief.

Sympathy never empathy.

Howls of the Wild

Coyotes howl against the sunset
prowling First Nation legends

Wolves howl against the moon
gathering a hungry pack

Jackals howl in the morning
building family bonds

Hounds howl anytime
chasing prey

Mothers howl in birth
celebrating life

Jeny howled in death
mourning her daughter

The Scales Favor Love Gained

"Tis better to have loved and lost" —Alfred Lord Tennyson

The loss of a daughter hurts

in direct proportion to love shared.

Sadly, family love

bodes agony in departure or death.

Each day is a gift to be opened

to the excitement of love and life,

to risk separation or death.

Everyone knows in the bowels of being

relationships end, but we hope

the joy of companionship

outweighs loss.

Happy the family, who live

apart in space and time, but

very close in spirit,

eager to share lives,

learning one from each other.

Over the years

valuing and honoring personal

energy and space.

Dare we

all care enough,

never give in to fear

death or departure,

living joyfully with the gift

of love and life, even in the

sunset of Dawn's

time.

No Escape

Warm cottage deck
invites peace, repose.

Imagination soars
in cushion comfort.

Cumulus fractals
form art and life,

eruptions, archipelagos,
mountain ranges.

At sunset we see a tear,
remember Dawn is no longer here.

Falling Leaves

In ancestral trees

roots deepen to unknown ends.

Limbs and branches form; leaflets sprout.

Some depart too early, awash in tears;

others linger until full colors fade

and fall in the fullness of their time.

If harsh winds howl

desperate leaves cling,

postpone death's sting,

but old and weak

sail on billowing gale.

Alas, no evergreen,

leaves descend.

Fall complete, the gatherer comes,

commits some to mulch,

casts some to fire.

Dawn ripped from the tree,

fallen leaf before her time.

Our hour to join is coming;

we feel the wind, our stems are frail;

how soon to the ground are we?

Two Urns Sit on the Shelf

(For Maryella and Wayne)

One for coffee

One for ashes

One for morning

One for mourning

One to see morning through a window pane

One to see mourning through daily pain

One to enjoy the sun

One to remember a son

II

In the first section I reflected on my direct interaction with grief. The following poems are about my personal journey beyond grief. Some involve Dawn, some do not. Hopefully sharing my developments and experiences sheds further insight into my management of loss and grief.

No Longer a Redskin. My high school has a strong commitment to First Nations' culture. For almost 90 years, with the approval of Native Americans at the time, we were known as the Redskins. With modern politics and a deeper understanding of the origins of the word, the nickname was dropped. My poem respects the change but acknowledges loss as a struggle.

Payday Reflections. The West was an important part of my formative years. Although my family was mostly farmers, Cowboy Poetry was a good mode to reflect the ethics and opinions of many of the people who helped shape me.

The Magnificence of Nothingness. When Dawn was two, we huddled in the shelter of our apartment basement while a Fujita 5 tornado devastated Topeka Kansas. The locals thought a large Native American burial mound on the southwest corner would protect the city. The tornado roared over the mound and through town from the southwest corner to the northeast. The shocking loss from something to nothing remains a strong memory.

Ode to an Old House (Circa 1857). From 1980 -1990, we lived in Normal, Illinois, and I taught at Illinois State University. Part of that time we lived in a big house built in 1857. We had students live with us in a Christian community. The time was very meaningful in the development of Dawn and our family.

Anonymous Angel. In 2017, I had a serious stroke. One experience during the rehabilitation was a tragic loss. The poem reflects the poignancy of that experience.

Hands of Reflection. I have lived my life with strong, positive relationships with people of different cultures. Cudjo Lewis, one of the last surviving slaves, is an important segment of history in Mobile. I observed Cudjo's hands in one of his pictures and was fascinated imagining the stories they could tell.

Sumo Bout with Doubt. My Christian faith has been central to my life for many years. My journey included wrestling with doubt.

Some Die a Lonely Death. The recent pandemic affected me in ways I did not expect. A close friend was dying of pancreatic cancer and the COVID quarantine isolated him. I tried to describe the isolation and fear of loss.

Dr. Sue Walker is a past Poet Laureate for Alabama. In her workshops she introduced many different forms of poetry. The next three poems are three different poetry forms, focused on broader topics. Two contain a reference to Dawn.

Cento: Livin' with Peace. In my opinion, a cento celebrates poetry in a similar manner as pastiche celebrates visual art.

Shape Poem: Bittersweet Tree. Dawn was generous with mementos, including Christmas ornaments. A shape poem conveys the bittersweet memories when Jeny decorates the tree.

Zuihitsu: Wandering in Place. I used the Zuihitsu form to relate moments in my life, including Dawn's death.

My wife and I always feel a special closeness when we travel internationally. That closeness helped us in our grieving processes. The final four poems are from our travels to Paris, to Northern Ireland and to Africa.

In the Rose Garden of Musée Rodin. Dawn's final professional trip was to Paris. She made a list of the things we were to do if we ever visited Paris. We went in part to honor her. We did everything on the list except stay at the very expensive hotel in which she stayed on a company expense account. The Rodin Garden was my favorite site.

A Long Time to Remember. On my first trip to Northern Ireland, the country was in the tail end of the "Troubles." My wife accompanied me on the next visit and we got to see the pageantry of July 12 under more peaceful circumstances.

Apartheid Absurdity. Our trip to South Africa was to be highlighted by a trip to Robbin Island where Nelson Mandela was imprisoned. High waves prevented our visit to the prison. Our disappointment was replaced with a charming and enlightening visit to a small museum.

Mandala Circles. On safari in South Africa, we encountered circles of life and death.

No Longer a Redskin

Redskin, a long-ago derogatory term,

for 80 years honored courage and strength,

a powerful force reducing First Nation prejudice.

Past tense bad, present tense good.

Past relates to affected people.

Past and affected people won.

Today meaningful parts of me were sacrificed for the sake of
others.

I make the sacrifice respectfully but acknowledge the pain of
loss.

Redskin— word reviled by some, revered by others.

Courage and strength gained by adoption

discolored by prejudice.

The joy of identification with a great culture

removed in honor of past pain.

Excitement of rhythms and color dim into the past.

Today meaningful parts of me were sacrificed for the sake of others.

I make the sacrifice respectfully but acknowledge the pain of loss.

For some, mascot is derision,

a negative caricature,

a focus for disdain.

For me, a positive image,

a meaningful symbol of a culture,

a leader into competition.

Today meaningful parts of me were sacrificed for the sake of others.

I make the sacrifice respectfully but acknowledge the pain of loss.

Unfortunately, eliminating words and symbols does not change hearts;

bigots find new words and symbols for hate.

Cancelation does not change prejudice.

Today meaningful parts of me were sacrificed for the sake of others.

I make the sacrifice respectfully but acknowledge the pain of loss.

He saddles-up occasionally but a Ram is his ride.

Well-worn chaps and rusty spurs hang on a post near the hay,

Stetson, seven-stitch boots, and brass belt-buckle worn with
pride,

in the dim-lit honky-tonk, on payday.

Singers never as purty as Dolly or as country as Hank,

 as loved as Willy or the whiskey he drank,

singing tunes made famous by others.

Years of longneck Buds and Camels

made for perfect smoke-rings with ease.

The old man rarely spoke,

but when he sat back and blew

everyone knew

he was ready to speak.

When he did, he was heard.

o   O   ◎   ◎

I seen plenty when I served in Nam—

blacks, Mexicans, Indians, Jews,

some country clods, some city dudes.

Reparations, microaggressions, cultural appropriations

I don't understand,

I keep it simple.

There's them with good hearts and them that's jerks,

and not much in between.

You gotta cull the good from the bad

and hope they do the same.

Any good heart walks through the door—

a handshake, a hug, I'll buy 'em a beer

and fight any man who shows disrespect.

A jerk is on his own.

o   O   ◎   ◎

Next you ride the prairie,

look high in the sky,

where the elite fly

looking down their noses at fly-over states.

They never prayed for rain to come,

never prayed for rain to go;

many never prayed.

Never baled hay, slopped hogs,

shucked corn or picked peas.

No manual labor for the jet set;

they live off others' sweat.

But from high on their horses

they righteously proclaim

what we can and cannot do.

We can't use certain words

because we might offend;

don't matter what we intend.

But it's okay for them to call us

hayseeds, crackers, hillbillies,

hicks, rednecks, honkies

bubbas, bumpkins, and peckerwoods.

Don't get all hep up about them;

they ain't worth the worry.

Save your energy for faith, family, and friends.

o   O   ◎   ◎

You're itchin' to leave small town life

for bright lights, busy nights.

I don't begrudge the change;

just don't judge us who stay

to see sunrise glory, feel sunset peace,

and reflect under the Milky Way.

o   O   ◎   ◎

You boys, sowin' oats, you need to learn

women ain't objects for gratification;

they're humans with feelings, hopes, and dreams.

If they want to work support'em,

if they look down their noses at mothers and wives,

give'em room.

If they're married stay away,

if they cuss to act tough, they are as dumb as men.

Don't git catawampus 'bout looks;

if they're hung up on purty, let'em be.

If you find one who is comfortable within her own skin,

who's honest and will work with you,

saddle up, get to work;

be honest with them.

See what you can build.

o   O   ◎   ◎

Love ain't just frolicking

though that's a good part.

It's doin' for her—

and appreciating what she's doin' for you.

It's working together on what's right.

o   O   ◎   ◎

If you have children,

teach'em to saddle and care for their own horses.

Give them plenty of rope,

raise them to live with someone else

from the day they're born.

When they make mistakes

(and they will)

make sure they accept responsibility,

experience consequences

and learn what is right.

Yelling what's wrong

won't do as much as showing what's right.

If they are falling,

(unless they are in danger)

let'em fall,

but giv'em a hand up.

Do not expect what you do not live.

Enjoy the ride,

they grow up fast.

o   O   ◎   ◎

If your needs are met

don't sweat the wants.

If you get some wants enjoy them,

but understand

they don't make you a better person.

No horse, no saddle, no boot, no buckle

helps you treat people better.

My trailer provides shelter

a bathroom, a kitchen with ample food,

a bed, a closet filled with clothes,

a television and comfy recliner.

My needs are met.

My truck

gets me from A to B,

holds hay and supplies.

My needs are met.

If I get better shelter, a better truck,

I will enjoy them,

but I'm not a better person.

o   O   ◎   ◎

Don't judge by the color of skin,

house size, fancy car, powerful truck,

amount of money or looks.

See how people care

for friends, for family, for their horses.

If they smile freely, listen to others,

say thank you and you're welcome,

then look them in their eyes,

shake their hands,

support them in bad times,

celebrate together in good times,

and build friendships that last.

The Magnificence of Nothingness

(Topeka, June 8, 1966)

Eerie silence in green heavens

bodes evil, spinning billows.

Sirens signal what Kansans already know— hide below.

Devastation forms on the distant prairie.

No hopping, skipping, jumping tail.

Pillar of thick and wide, lowers and levels,

then howls and devours a long swath

from field to town and beyond.

Within the disturbed sacred burial site

one hears the cry— "no protection here"—

as destruction roars over Burnett's mound

and rumbles down through town.

Miles and minutes pass in fury

until curious calm returns to splinters of oblivion

and air replaces matter.

Perished images mock unbelief;

silence pays homage to frightening power.

In quiet awe and dread-filled discomfort,

we see the magnificence of nothingness.

Ode to an Old House (Circa 1857)

Your site, an effortless selection,

highest, driest an obvious choice

for a farmer needing a home.

Shovel by shovel,

bucket by bucket,

a basement emerged.

Heavy fieldstone-lined edges,

time passes, but you

retain a firm foundation.

Hand-hewn heart of pine beams

aged hard as steel

still hold you on their backs.

Your cupola recalls and smiles

seeing

    Lincoln and his top hat trotting by,

    the town and university growing,

    first planes barnstorming

hearing

> Douglas orating

> first cars chugging

> first phone ringing

feeling

> first electricity surging,

> first indoor plumbing flushing,

> central air modulating.

Your halls and walls expanded
as cars replaced horses;
the kitchen needed space,
and bathrooms sought privacy.

120 years after your birth, irony strikes—
a psychologist moved
into the old house
on Main Street
in a town called Normal.

"This old house once knew my children
This old house once knew my wife
This old house was home and shelter
as we fought the storms of life"

Students joined the family;

a community formed

amid song, prayer, fun, love.

"This old house once rang with laughter

This old house heard many shouts"

40 years later, despite dispersion,

community love retains connections

and endures on a firm foundation.

Quotes are from *This Old House* by Stuart Hamblen

Anonymous Angel

Drab rehab challenges spirits,

fear attacks survivors,

some fight in hope,

others recoil within.

She was a hopeful fighter,

face lined by time,

and many racial scars,

bearing no barrier to my whiteness.

Knotted kerchief framed twinkling eyes;

her infectious smile lifted hearts, brightened the gym.

Session over, I wheeled away.

She broadly beamed and gently waved.

That night she died.

I never knew her name.

Cudjoe Lewis

Clotilda survivor, one of the last living slaves.

Grainy photos reveal Rodin-worthy hands:

thumbs sculpted like small plantains

aligned with strong, gnarled fingers

and a missing fingertip!

Your hands

firmly grip legacies

of seizure, passage, servitude, freedom

with a fingertip left behind.

Your hands

fought captors in Benin,

touched hopelessness bounding the wretched sea,

toiled beneath the scourge of slavery,

joyfully folded with peals of liberty.

Your hands

magnificent sculpted hands,

reflections of the worst of humanity

honor to the best.

Sumo Bout with Doubt

Cancer comes quietly,

a daughter dies loudly

undeniable realities.

After numerous skirmishes

the paramount battle is fought,

triggered by fear and loss.

A Sumo bout in the dohyo of the mind,

Rikishi of belief battles Rikishi of disbelief.

Bow, take stances, collide.

A colossal confrontation,

thundering power,

tsunamis on brain's beaches.

Synaptic fireworks explode as the Fourth,

dendrites rattle as San Andreas' quakes,

aftershock after aftershock after aftershock.

Past the Forbidden Wall

in deep pits and dark crevices

slithers Thomas doubt.

Denial beckons beyond Peter,

not once or twice or thrice,

but forever and always,

battling neither a Christmas nor Easter nod,

not an emotional altar call,

but belief woven in fiber.

Peter denied as Jesus died,

later Thomas doubted,

fear of death drove life.

From fright and unbelief

to good news, even martyr's deaths;

they must have seen something.

Final bow,

Shiroboshi belief and Yokozuna,

Kuroboshi disbelief.

Glossary: Sumo: form of Japanese wrestling
Dohyo: wrestling circle within which a match occurs
Rikishi: wrestler
Shiroboshi: winner
Yokozuna: grand champion
Kuroboshi: loser

Some Die a Lonely Death

Death imagined: old age, comfortable, amid family, friends;

reality strikes imagination cold.

Some die young--some in pain--some alone.

My friend in isolation is old--not in pain--but solitary,

more than solitary, shaken, feeling forsaken.

facing the most desolate death of all, staring at a wall

in virus quarantine with untouchable love nearby.

Family in the parking lot, facing death without a funeral—

like the first birthday without the daughter who died too young.

Tech wisps and glimpses insufficient.

Pray for release— to touch, to joy, to love,

before release takes love home forever.

Livin' with Peace

"When I have fears that I may cease to be,[1] down in the sounding foam of primal things I reach my hands and play with pebbles of destiny.[2] Though all the fates should prove unkind,[3] I guess I will live on. I could've died for love— but for livin' I was born.[4]

When the wind stirs soft through the springing grass,[5] and life is too much like a pathless wood,[6] I know that I shall meet my fate somewhere among the clouds above.[7] I shall have peace, as leafy trees are peaceful.[8]"

1. "When I have fears that I may cease to be" John Keats
2. "Who am I" Carl Sandburg
3. "Though all the Fates" Henry David Thoreau
4. "Life is Fine" Langston Hughes
5. "Sympathy" Ralph Laurence Dunbar
6. "The Road Not Taken" Robert Frost
7. "An Irish Airman Meets His Fate" W. B. Yeats
8. "I Shall not Care" Sara Teasdale

Bittersweet Tree

Star

Angels

Candlestick

Chipped Turtle

Wooden Figurines

Granny's Santa; She's Gone

Mom's Tiny Mouse; She's Gone

Hand Painted Clowns, Ceramic Elves

Homemade Crosses; Grandchildren Memories

Bells, Star Fish, Hat, Trombone, Miniature Eiffel Tower

Daughter's Many Baubles; She Was Taken, Apples, Lace Angel

King Herod, Brown Bear, Red Balls, More Angels, Hot Air Balloon

Wooden Angel Fish, Cowboy Boots, Tragedy Mask

Happy Past Contrasts the Now

Trimming Joy, Often in Tears

Wandering in Place

Lightning strikes, thunder roars

and wisteria wafts in the breeze

Mansel died from cancer after flying into the fight against forest fires.

I hear the ambulance for Nancy, the morning she had a seizure and
died.

Sleeping outdoors on cots

the basement is alive with children dancing.

Big dipper bops to rock and roll

and I can only dance the waltz

Feet so narrow, my dress shoes were Girl Scout oxfords.

Friends at Woodland Methodist never knew my secrets.

When the bobber drops, the campfire flairs

and work seems far away.

Sliding a concrete banister frayed my new jeans.

Winter's potholes loomed through the rusted floorboard of my '42
Ford.

Walking the Royal Gorge Bridge frightens,
hearing rain on my tin roof calms.

When a doctor says "Come see your baby boy, he needs surgery,"
you go.

Unknown to us, our apartment was owned by a distant cousin.

Three children in a trailer are a lot to ask of a wife.

The chicken we served was actually Thumper.

The net over the Koi Pond keeps herons away.

A puppy tugs your heart, until he eats your shoes.

A psychologist living on Main Street in Normal is not normal.

The community of young who lived with us are now old.

I love the mountains, she loves the beach

We sold the cabin and bought a gulf cottage

My fall and winter lived in the eternal summer of Alabama.

Come to Byron Center, bury your daughter; she was killed today.

In the Rose Garden of Musée Rodin

i

Louvre's dim halls

brightened by Mona and Monet

brighter yet, Musée d'Orsay --

my struggle . . . yet to come.

ii

In rich sunlight shone

two luring Thinkers—

one large among the roses,

one small amid the damned.

Circles of Inferno

sculpted pain in bronze,

lust-less nakedness

overwhelming doom.

The Shade's shadows cover hopelessness,

high souls of the condemned,

Les Trois Hombres abutting . . . but apart

umbrae in isolation.

Molded in forged gates,

I see shrieks of agony,

know Meditation's horror,

feel everlasting Despair.

Depraved, wicked, evil

embedded before my eyes;

Ugolino, saint of cannibalism

leads savages into Hell.

Being a brother's keeper

doesn't mean sleeping with his wife—

Paolo, saint of debauchery

leads lechers into Hell,

and twisted, fallen Caryatid

burdened not by good,

crushed by boulder load—

no escape, no hope

III

Before a brooding Thinker

I reflect, I ponder,

then imagine other gates

cast for other fates.

Covered by a quilt of guilt,

lapses hide among my clutter,

attach to anxieties and fears,

grow tentacles to harm.

Light blinds anxieties clinging

to darkest corners of my mind

and melts fear's bergs blocking

love's flow to joy and life.

Below a brooding Thinker,

seek the light how one may,

in deep meditation— humbly I pray

until illuminated, forgiven, free.

Enlightenment entrusted;

from massive doors I turn

amid soft petals and Rose wafts,

breathe hope . . . see beauty . . . feel love.

iv

If ever one chooses

reflection before Hell's gloom,

contemplation is suggested

when roses reign in bloom.

A Long Time to Remember

Along thorny hedges and grassy lea,

my ancestors' Antrim flows to the sea.

Along the Giant's Causeway, hear

July Twelve echoes every year.

Pipes and drums lead each Orange march

through village squares and by the larch.

Bushmills fuels fun and schemes,

and bonfires flame Ulster dreams.

Battle of Boyne fought long ago

remembered in village and borough.

In times of trouble— provocation

In times of peace— celebration.

May "The Troubles" always cease

and each remember the joy of peace.

Apartheid Absurdity

Table Mountain splendor, grand and clean from far away,

but close in Table Bay, sordid history lies in Robben's woeful cries:

apartheid pain, Mandela's confinement.

Our crown jewel event, canceled by high waves,

replaced by a quaint museum on Buitenkamp street.

Resident guides keep history alive, telling tales of District Six.

Hindis, Christians, Muslims, and Jews

living peacefully together despite differing views.

Apartheid required demolition to deny successful integration.

Our guide, a wee brown man with twinkling eyes,

a Nehru jacket, a crochet skull cap,

shared pictures with pride, then told an interesting tale.

On a bench on display with a Whites Only sign,

our guide saw a white man seated.

He reflected; "what makes him better than me?"

Then noted, beside the man sat his pet.

Our guide exploded; "how can this possibly be? How is a dog better than me?"

Then with a wry smile and a wink, he leaned in and cackled – "and his dog was black!"

He laughed in glee.

at apartheid absurdity.

The museum was good to see.

Mandala Circles

The radio crackles,

the guide cries,

"We've got a kill,"

as we speed through eventide

to lionesses circled in sleep, full and deep,

while once proud manes partake alms.

Giraffe's death no accident,

run down, circled, torn asunder.

As we depart,

circling hyenas slink apart

settle in remnant wait.

Vulture silhouettes

circle before the moon,

terminal scavengers picking orts.

Tomorrow will be as mandala blown,

as the pride returns to prey

and death and life circle another day.